A Straightforward Guide to Teaching Your Child to Swim

Louise Fyfe

ABOUT THE AUTHOR

Louise Fyfe is Editor of SPORT, the magazine of the Sports Council. She writes extensively on a number of sports, health and fitness issues, and is author of Careers in Sport, published by Kogan Page.

Straightforward Publishing Limited
38 Cromwell Road, London E17 9JN

© Louise Fyfe
   First Edition 1995

British Library Cataloguing in Publication data. A catalogue record for this book is available from the British Library.

ISBN 0–9521153–3–6

Printed by BPC Wheaton—Exeter
Cover design & illustrations by Neil Grant, Front Line Graphics, Gerrard Street, Brighton

CONTENTS

LIST OF ILLUSTRATIONS

INTRODUCTION

Swimming is not only a fun activity for children, it is excellent for all-round health and essential for personal safety near water. This straightforward handbook aims to provide parents with practical information on getting started, safety, ideas on how to help your child gain water confidence and, ultimately, learn the basic strokes.

It is important to remember that all the exercises described in this book are intended for use only in a controlled environment—the public swimming pool. The water is clear, you can watch your child at all times and there are no unseen dangers such as rocks or strong currents which can be encountered in open water such as rivers, the sea, reservoirs, lakes or canals. Do not carry out any of these exercises in open water because of these hazards. Play safe and take your child to the local swimming pool.

In addition, there is invaluable advice for the professional or budding professional teacher on general pool health, safety and hygiene. This will enable you to create the conditions necessary to ensure that the swimming environment is safe and secure.

For ease of reference throughout the book, the feminine gender has been used to refer to your child.

1

OUT OF THE WATER

WHY SHOULD YOUR CHILD LEARN TO SWIM?

Quite simply, because swimming is fun and there is a whole new watery world out there for your child to enjoy. It's never too late to teach your child to swim, but the younger the child, the more readily she will accept water as a natural place to be.

At a very early age children may not have developed a fear of the water, and as they have already had nine months in the womb in a fluid environment, it's generally thought that they will feel very natural and at ease in a swimming pool. However, it would be unwise to take a child of less than six months to a pool, not least because she will become very chilled very quickly. To keep her water confidence high, you can play games with your baby in the bath at home.

If toddlers or older children are more apprehensive about learning to swim, to help them overcome their fears, make sure that a visit to the pool—and simply being in the water—is a thoroughly enjoyable experience.

Your ultimate aim, however, as a parent, must be to see your child swim unaided, confidently and safely for the reasons outlined below.

- **Personal safety**

The ability to swim is essential for every child's safety, and for her parents' peace of mind. As a parent, you must be confident that if your child were to enter deep water accidentally and unsupervised, she would have a chance to survive. It is estimated that one quarter of the deaths by drowning that occur in England and Wales are children under the age of fifteen. Such statistics could be dramatically reduced if children learnt to swim when they learnt to walk, rather than waiting until the average age of seven to nine years, or in many cases until much later in life.

- **To keep fit and healthy**

How often do you hear people comment that they feel fitter and fresher after a swim? Your child will feel the same. The best kind of exercise is one which benefits all the body systems and functions, and there is no activity which does that more effectively than swimming. The Allied Dunbar National Fitness Survey reported that people who exercise regularly as children are more likely to continue to exercise in later years. It also reported a clear association between lack of participation in sport and physical recreation from an early age and the prevalence of heart disease, angina and breathlessness. By teaching your child to swim, and encouraging her to visit the pool regularly, you'll be instilling a pattern of exercise in her that will have proven health benefits in years to come.

• To participate in other water sports

As Rat says in 'The Wind in the Willows', there's absolutely nothing half so much worth doing as simply messing about in boats on the river. And he's right. Teaching your child to swim will allow them to take part confidently and safely in a wide range of water sports. Canoeing, surfing, sailing, water skiing, snorkelling and rafting—they are all exhilarating sports that provide hours of fun, but they all carry the pre-requisite that participants, children and adults, must be able to swim confidently and comfortably.

• For family fun

Swimming is one of the few sports that all members of a family can enjoy together—whether they are sixty or six months. With the advent of leisure pools, flumes and water attractions, a family swim can be a fun affair that doesn't cost the earth.

With more families taking holidays, and particularly

activity holidays, than ever before, the opportunities are endless if your whole family can swim.

NON-SWIMMING PARENTS

It is not essential for a parent to be able to swim to take a baby or a child into the water, providing they stay where they themselves feel happy and only in a shallow pool. If possible, a non-swimming parent should at least learn to both float and to regain a standing position, with their feet on the bottom of the pool, so that should they slip while holding the child they can immediately recover themselves. A lot of public pools hold parent-toddler classes enabling both to learn to swim together. In these classes, a qualified teacher will help you to guide the child through the stages towards learning to swim, which will, in turn, help you to get used to the water. The best advice, however, is to learn to swim yourself through a qualified instructor before taking your child to swim. Not only will you feel happier about being in the water with your child but you will also be able to pass on your new found skills to her. Also bear in mind that any tension you feel in the water will be passed on to your child. If she sees that you are nervous, she too will become tense, and may pick up your fear of the water.

WHAT EQUIPMENT DOES YOUR CHILD NEED?

Swimming is one of the few activities that requires little in the way of expensive equipment. A swimming costume or trunks, a swimming aid, a towel, some toiletries and a kit bag are all that's needed. Rinse everything out afterwards in cold water so that the chlorine from the pool doesn't rot a favourite costume.

• Swimwear

Proper close-fitting swimwear that your child feels comfortable in and likes wearing is a must. It must be stretchy to allow a wide range of movement. Babies and toddlers should not wear a nappy. Before you go check out whether or not the pool that you are visiting insists that swimmers with long hair wear a cap.

• Swimming aids

Swimming aids come in a variety of forms, shapes and colours and the use of buoyancy aids really depends on your personal preference. There is little doubt that you will feel more confident if your child has some kind of initial support. It is important, however, to gradually reduce the child's reliance upon the aids, to avoid over dependence. If they are worn, allow the child to enter the water for a short time without them, put the swimming aids on during the majority of time in the water, and remove the swimming aids at the end of the session to allow the child some freedom and time to attempt to swim without them.

Armbands

These develop early confidence and independence in the child as she can happily bob around in the knowledge that she will stay afloat and her head will remain above the water. A major advantage is that the bands can be blown up to fit the child's arm securely. The most effective ones have two parallel chambers that go right round the arm with no flat side, as these give the most support. There are plans to bring in a British Standard for armbands. When you are buying them ask if this type is available. While wearing armbands, a child can use all her limbs and begin to co-ordinate swimming movements. As water confidence grows, you can reduce the amount of air in the bands until the child is happily swimming without any support. Ensure that your child's armbands are properly maintained—rinse the chlorine off them after use and keep them safely away from sharp objects likely to puncture them.

Rubber rings

These are not appropriate for use while teaching your child to swim. Rubber rings cannot be blown up to fit around a child securely and tend to end up around the child's waist. Although they do encourage a horizontal position, the main danger of this method of support is that when the child is horizontal, the ring can tend to slip to their lower body and make the body top heavy thus pushing the head into the water and the feet into the air—a very dangerous position.

Buoyancy suits

Buoyancy suits are swimming costumes with sewn-in polystyrene buoyancy. Like rings, they also encourage a more horizontal position, but they have the advantage over rings in that the buoyance tends to be around the chest rather than the waist, and the buoyancy is secure in that it is sewn into the costume. They also enable free body movement and thus all the limbs can be used and co-ordination can be improved.

Floats

Again, hand-held polystyrene floats encourage a horizontal body position and allow kicking skills and leg co-ordination to develop. However, they are best used for children with some experience as they have to be held in the hand for support. They do not allow for the simultaneous co-ordination of arm and leg movements.

HOW DO YOU CHOOSE A SWIMMING POOL?

Although the advent of leisure pools has enabled millions of children to have a lot of fun in the water, many of them are not geared to actual swimming, and wave machines, water slides and fountains can be distracting to the child. Look for a traditional pool in your area that also has either a toddlers pool or a teaching pool. If your children are older, they will be able to use most pools provided they can touch the pool bottom at the shallow end.

Local papers are likely to have details and advertisments for swimming pools in your area, as well as private clubs and leisure centres.

Use of floats

THE POOL

To make the first visit an enjoyable and positive an experience for you and your child, check on the following by making a pre-swimming visit if possible:

• Is there a separate toddlers or teaching pool ?

• Are the water depths and safety instructions clearly marked?

• If there is only one pool, how shallow is the shallow end? Will your child be able to stand up in it?

• Is the water temperature on display? Preferably it should be about 27C / 80F.

• If chlorine affects you or your child, does the pool use ozone as a water purifier?

• At what times is the swimming pool open to the public? What are the pool's peak times? Swimming at the time when the pool is quietest will be more helpful to you and less distracting to your child.

- Is there permanent lifeguard cover? Some private clubs do not always provide a lifeguard or attendant. Do the poolside staff seem alert? Lifeguards are there to look out for people or children doing things which might be dangerous.

- Does the pool offer a programme of swimming lessons? If possible, find a pool that has parent and children lessons.

THE CHANGING FACILITIES

The swimming pool itself is not the only facility you will use on your visit. It is also worthwhile checking on the changing facilities:

- Are the changing areas clean and warm? Are they supervised?

- Are the lockers big enough for your and your child's clothes or will you need two? How secure are the lockers?

- Is there somewhere safe to leave your buggy or pushchair?

- Is there a changing facility for parents with babies and toddlers? Does the changing room have changing tables, nappy bins and a playpen for you to put your child in while you dress/undress?

- Are there family changing rooms? These are large cubicles where you can change as a family. They make it easier for mothers on their own with young sons and fathers on their own with daughters. If no such facility exists, ask the staff what arrangements can be made for you.

- Can you take your child's towel onto the poolside?

- Are there adequate numbers of toilet and shower units?

It is also worth checking out the cost of swimming as this can vary considerably from pool to pool. Some pools charge more during school holidays and at weekends. Other pools may have fun slides and wave machines which may put the admission price up.

Although a swim can cost an adult up to £3.00, most pools charge considerably less for children and in some cases those under three years go in free. Most pools have concessions for those who are on income support or who are unemployed.

HYGIENE

Ensure that your child is aware of the role of hygiene at a swimming pool. The provision of toilet and shower facilities is not only for your own benefit, but for the community at large. The prevention of the spread of infection is every pool user's responsibility, and personal cleanliness makes an important contribution. Make sure you and your child have visited the toilet and showered before entering the pool.

Chapter 4 offers more advice on general pool health, safety and hygiene.

Now please read the KEY POINTS from chapter 1 opposite.

KEY POINTS

- It is unwise to take a child of less than six months to a pool.

- It is preferable, although not essential, for a parent to be able to swim to take a child into the water. However, it is advisable to learn how to float.

- Initially, you may feel more confident if your child wears some form of swimming aid for support. It is important, however, to gradually reduce the child's reliance upon aids, to avoid over-dependence.

- Before making your first visit to the pool, you should make a pre-swimming visit to check conditions are acceptable.

2

IN THE WATER

When you first arrive at the pool it is worth walking around to make sure you know where the deep and shallow water is. Check the depth of the water before you take your child in. Make sure you go in at the shallow end if the pool is graduated. Once in the water, never turn your back on your child or leave her unattended at any point.

In the first few visits, you will not be attempting to teach the child proper strokes in any detail. You should simply allow your child to gain confidence in the water and encourage her to move around with ease. Make sure you are relaxed, as any fear you have will be picked up by the child. It is meant to be fun for both of you! Keep the session short to begin with—fifteen minutes may well be enough for the first time. You can always gradually increase this up to half an hour. Watch out for signs of coldness— shivering and blueness. If your child starts to suffer either of these, you should get out and make the child warm.

If your child is timid about getting into the pool, maybe on the first visit she could simply sit on the side and watch other children enjoying themselves. You could take her favourite bathtime toy along to make her feel more at home.

Once you take your child into the water, keep down at her level, even if it means kneeling on the bottom of the pool, and maintain eye contact with her to keep her confidence high. Make the experience as happy as possible by chatting and pointing out funny and interesting things at the pool.

Don't take your child into the water if she is suffering from a sniffly cold or bad chest, and certainly not if she has any ear trouble or eye infection.

GETTING YOUR CHILD USED TO THE WATER

CHILDREN UNDER SIX MONTHS

Do not take a new born baby to any public place until she has received some sort of immunization. Your doctor will advise you on what is necessary.

There are a number of things a parent can do at home to get their baby or toddler happy with the water and safe in it. Everything should be done gradually and gently, and should be fun. Babies and children learn better if they are enjoying themselves.

One of the best ways to start your child on their way to swimming is to encourage her to play in the bath at home. Encourage face and hair wetting and splashing around to get her used to the feeling of water on her body. Let her lie on her front stretched out with her chin on the water, and her hands on the bath bottom to practise kicking her legs. This can also be done while she is lying on her back. Make sure the bath is not too deep so that when she is lying on her back her ears are under water but her mouth and face are clear of the surface. If a baby's head does go under the water, most will become upset and open their mouths to cry. This will mean they will swallow water which will, in turn, make them cough and choke. This could frighten the child who may never want to go near water again.

Show your child how to blow bubbles in the water. This is an essential skill and is the first stage in learning to breathe correctly when swimming. Do remember that you should never leave a child unattended in the bath, no matter how shallow the water.

FROM SIX TO EIGHT MONTHS

From about six months you can take your child to a pool, but don't keep her in the water for long as she will quickly become cold. Always ensure that the child is supported with your hands under her armpits and that her face is kept clear of the water.

At this stage you can teach your child how to blow proper bubbles in the water. First of all, show your baby what you want her to do, and then get her to do it. One way of doing this is to blow on the baby's face so that she feel the air and she also takes a breath in. Then gently submerge her face for less than a second and back up again. This is a gentle movement and is all over very quickly. Stop if your baby doesn't blow bubbles, or doesn't like it. Again, make sure it's a fun experience for you and the child.

FROM EIGHT MONTHS TO ABOUT TWO AND A HALF YEARS

This age group should be getting used to the water and starting the basics for swimming. Again, make your child feel generally confident in the water by holding her under the armpits and splashing her gently or bouncing her up and down in the water. At this stage you should get her used to having her face wet for a short time.

If there are two of you in the water with your toddler you can start to get ready for swimming with push and glide exercises. Both adults should stand close together. The adult holding the child should pass her on her front to the other adult ensuring that the baby's chin is on the water and her head held up. The child will glide over the surface to the other adult. The second adult should be facing the child to catch her. Push and glide exercises help children to stretch out in the water and get into the swimming position. Over a period of weeks you can start doing more as your child gains confidence. The two adults can gradually move apart though there should never be more than two metres between them and you can let the baby's nose and mouth fall into the water briefly to emphasise the importance of breathing out.

If your child can get used to the water by being on her back this has the advantage of her not getting her face in the water, and once children are happy on their back, they can learn to do more. However, not all children like being on their back in the water, particularly if they have just learned to sit up. They may try to sit up in the water. Children will get more water in their ears this way—a feeling they often dislike. You can help your child glide on her back in a swimming pool by putting her head on your shoulder and by pointing things out on the ceiling to look at.

If you can get your child to relax on her back, then start getting her to use her legs. With your baby's head on your shoulder, hold her knees and encourage her to kick with her legs. Kicking should be from the hips with straight legs but floppy feet.

To get your child's arms going, take along a ball or a floating bath-time toy. Hold your baby under the armpits and put the toy out in front of her. Get her to reach for the toy. This will begin to get her arms going. You can do this without holding her under the arms if she is wearing armbands.

FROM ABOUT TWO AND A HALF TO FIVE YEARS

As long as the child's feet can touch the bottom of the pool, you can get her ready for swimming by doing exercises with you standing a few feet away. Children of this age are likely to be able to concentrate for longer and can understand more. At this stage you can help her to use her arms, start to kick with her legs and get used to using floats rather than armbands.

Get your child to walk across the pool towards you while practising front paddle and keeping her arms under the water. She should keep one arm outstretched while pulling the other back towards her tummy. Her hands should be cupped, and the straight arm pulled in as the other is pushed back out. If your child is wearing armbands then she might also practise kicking for a short time.

To practise leg kicking, get your child to hold two

floats, one supporting each arm. The arms should be at either side of the body in a bent position. To begin with you might also hold the child under the forearms. The child should try to kick up and down with straight legs and floppy feet. Stay in front of your child at all times and keep looking at her and talking to her. Your child could also hold onto the rail and practise kicking her legs for a very short period of time.

To put the two together, try to encourage your child to hold onto the side rail and then push herself towards you, standing only a few feet away. She will glide for that few feet. If your child stretches out as much as possible she will get the feel for the swimming position. Gradually increase the distance so that the child has to start to paddle and kick to reach you. At this stage she is getting towards the first stages of swimming.

MOVEMENT IN THE WATER

Your child should be encouraged to move freely in the water from as early as possible. Get her to walk around the shallow end of the pool using the rail or the side, then get her to do the same exercise but without touching the rail. When she is confident about moving freely in the water, get her to walk as quickly as possible, in a variety of directions, or in a set pattern. Also encourage her to move with her shoulders under the water. When she feels comfortable with these exercises get her to experiment with hopping and jumping, and moving backwards and forwards. Follow the leader and tag are good games that will not only instill even greater confidence in your child in the water but will also prove to be good fun!

GETTING IN AND OUT OF THE POOL

Once your child is confident enough to move out of the teaching pool and into the shallow end of the main pool, she should be encouraged, if possible, to get herself in and out of the water. Early on, show her how to use the ladder type steps and emphasise that she must climb down facing the steps. Go down first and wait in the water directly below the steps. Similarly, show her how to climb out, then get back in the water and wait until she has been successful. For added confidence your child should be wearing her swimming aids at this time.

When your child is confident using the steps, another method of entering the water is from the poolside. She should sit on the side, feet in the water, and place both hands on the poolside to one side of her body. She should then turn to face her hands and slide in feet first. Again,

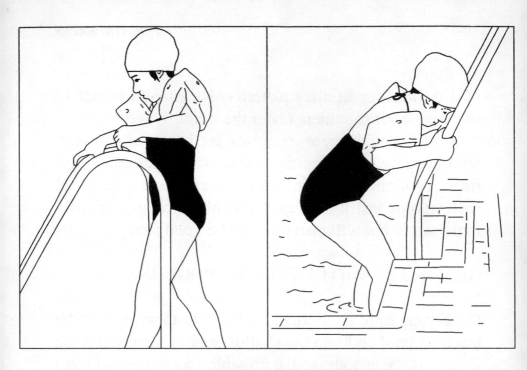

wait in the water directly below her until she is comfortable with this method of entry.

Jumping is every water-confident child's favoured method of entering the water! Initially, she should jump from a crouching position towards you in the water, making sure she enters the water feet first. You should reach out to support her on her entry into the water. As she gains more confidence she will happily jump into the water without you watching, providing she knows her feet will touch the bottom when she stands up. Emphasise to your child that this is also a controlled method of entering the water and should not be done recklessly, but from a crouching or standing position on the poolside.

Do not try to teach your child to dive into the pool. Diving is a complex and potentially dangerous activity and should be taught by a knowledgeable and experienced teacher and in a swimming pool with suitable water depth and forward clearance.

You should teach your child to climb out at the side of the pool, by putting her hands on the side, pushing up and swinging her knee onto the side. The steps can be used, if she finds this too physically demanding.

INTRODUCING THE SWIMMING ACTIONS

As your child comes to terms with water and begins to enjoy herself through a variety of activities, the need to work on an effective method of moving through the water will naturally grow.

From the side wall or rail, get your child to push her body towards you, arms stretched out. You should be standing a few feet away, and should increase your distance the more confident your child becomes. After practising this, let your child stand a few feet from the side and push her body, arms stretched out, and glide towards it. Gradually increase the distance so that your child has to kick her legs to reach the side. Ensure she keeps her chin on the water. At this stage, she is getting towards the first stages of beginning to swim. She will probably still be using some kind of swimming aid. If it is of the inflatable variety, it would be a good idea to gradually decrease the amount of air inside as her confidence grows.

Encourage your child to get as close to horizontal as possible. It is likely that the leg movements she will find easiest will be the up and down alternating kick associated with front crawl swimming. At the same time, try to encourage her to paddle with her arms. This stroke is now known as the front paddle, but is probably better known to

Introducing the swimming actions

you as the doggy paddle. If your child can do this she's just done her first swimming strokes!

THE FRONT PADDLE STROKE

For your child to carry out front paddle you must be aware of the following:

• **The child's body position**

The body should be as near to horizontal as possible. In the early learning stages your child will probably swim with her head up. Later, as her confidence increases, she can lower her face into the water, thus making her position in the water more horizontal.

• **The leg action**

Your child's legs should be stretched out and as close to the horizontal as possible. The kick should start at the hip, and travel down through the knee and the stretched ankle to the stretched toes. Her legs should be kept as straight as possible, though some bending at the knee is likely. As one leg is moving down, the other should be moving up. The upward movement should end when the heel breaks

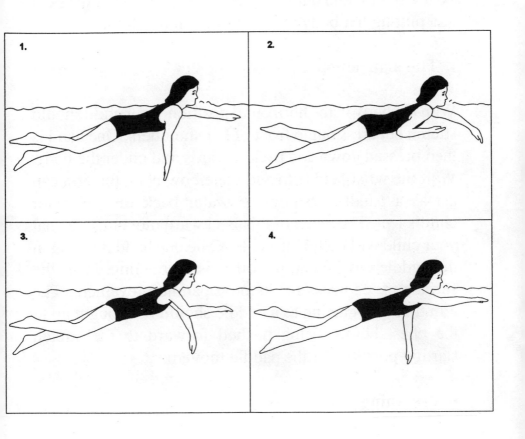

The front paddle

the surface of the water. This leg action is called the alternating kick and can be easily practised by getting your child to hold onto the side rail or the side of the pool and putting her body in the horizontal position.

• The arm action

With the body in the horizontal position, your child should stretch her arms out in front of her shoulders. One hand is then pressed down and back towards and under the body. With the wrist held firm and the elbow bent, the arm can act as a paddle pushing the water back towards your child's feet. The result of this backward movement is that your child will travel forward. While one hand is acting in the paddle movement, the other is recovering under the surface in readiness for its next paddle movement. The arm that is not acting as a paddle should be brought up to the chest before being pushed forward to the stretch starting position for the paddle movement.

• Breathing

At this stage, your child's breathing techniques are not that important. Natural survival instincts ensure that air comes from somewhere! However, if you do want to emphasise any particular aspect of breathing, try to get her to breathe out vigorously.

• Co-ordination

Don't try to get your child to do too much at once. If she is staying afloat, and is happy, then make sure she understands the importance of maintaining the movements above rather than trying to get her to co-ordinate her legs and arms. At this stage the emphasis should still be on fun!

THE BACK PADDLE STROKE

• Body position

As near horizontal as possible. Your child's body should be straight, with the back of the head resting on the water, with her eyes looking directly upwards or slightly towards the feet. To keep this position, your child will have to keep her hips up.

• Leg action

The kick is again initiated at the hips and should travel through the knees and ankles to the toes. Each leg should again be kicked alternately. The upward movement is completed when the toes break the water's surface. Encourage your child to keep their legs straight and long, but, as in the front paddle, there will inevitably be some bend.

• Arm action

This involves the child's hands going through a figure of eight motion. Initially, your child may find it easier to make large sweeping movements with her arms—moving them in towards her body with force and back out again gently—to about 45 degrees from her body. The hands should be cupped as they are pushed in towards the body, and flat as they are gently moved out. As your child gains more confidence, the elbows should be kept closer to the body so that much of the movement is in the wrists. The most efficient way to use the hands is in a figure of eight motion just above or close to the thighs. Starting with her palms facing down, your child should then press them into the water while moving them towards the body. As they reach the body the hands should be turned face up and moved back to an angle of about 45 degrees from the body. At this point they should again be turned face down and the sequence repeated. This figure of eight action is

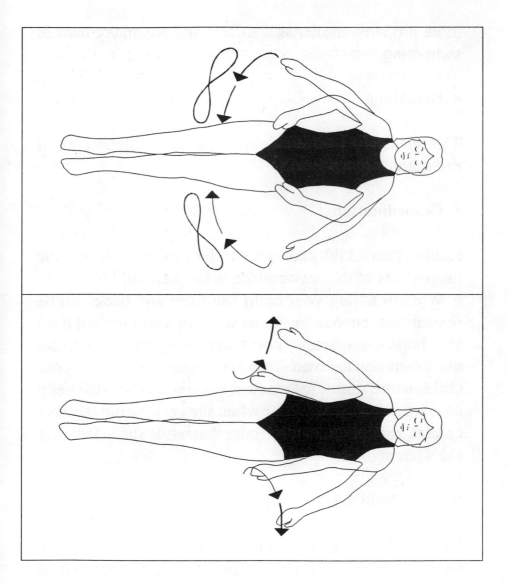

The back paddle

more properly known as sculling, and has many uses in swimming.

- **Breathing**

This should not be a problem as the face is always out of the water.

- **Co-ordination**

Ensure your child knows that she has to maintain the movements of the back paddle to keep afloat!

While teaching your child the front and back paddle movements, encourage her to wear a swimming aid until she feels completely comfortable carrying out the movements on her own. These movements may take your child some time to master, so remember to keep encouraging her, praise her when she gets the movements correct, and above all make sure that while she is learning she's having fun!

STANDING IN THE WATER

Once your child is joining in activities which require the feet to be off the bottom of the pool, it is important that, at

Standing

To regain the standing position

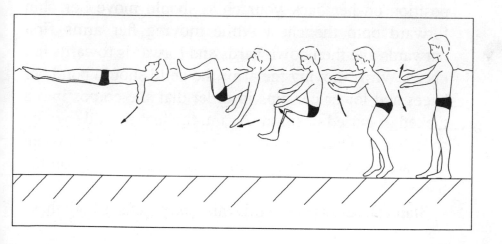

the same time, she learns how to regain the standing position. In the early stages of learning, your child may well panic while trying to stand up if the action does not happen smoothly.

For your child to stand on her feet from the front horizontal position involves the following moves. The child should raise her head then move both hands at once in the downward paddle position. As the hands reach the knees, which will be following the laws of gravity and falling downwards too, the knees should be brought forward under the body in a tucked position. The feet should then be stretched down towards the bottom of the pool and, when they are below the body, should be put on the bottom firmly.

To regain the standing position from a horizontal position on her back your child should move her chin forward onto the chest while moving her arms first outwards and then downwards and forwards towards her knees. While moving the arms the child should bend her knees and lower her hips in order that she comes into a tucked or curled position. Again, the feet should then be stretched down towards the bottom of the pool and, when they are below the body, should be placed firmly on the bottom.

Stand close by your child while she practises both these

moves in the shallow end of the pool. She initially only needs to be up to her waist in water to carry them out successfully.

TREADING WATER

The aim of treading water is to enable swimmers to maintain a stationary position out of their depth with their head above the water. Although your child may be able to swim, it does not necessarily follow that she can safely tread water out of her depth. A child who swims confidently in the shallow end can easily panic when faced with maintaining a stationary position at the surface in the deep end. The transition into deep water can be traumatic and you should only teach your child how to do it with great caution and if you are capable of rescuing her should she panic. Treading water is both a survival and self-rescue skill and it is important to make sure your child can do it successfully before she swims in deep water.

There are three main ways to tread water. Keeping the body vertical, with the arms below the water and moving in a front paddle action, your child should with cycle her legs, do short scissor kicks ensuring that her legs are kept straight, or move her legs in a breaststroke action. Practise

41

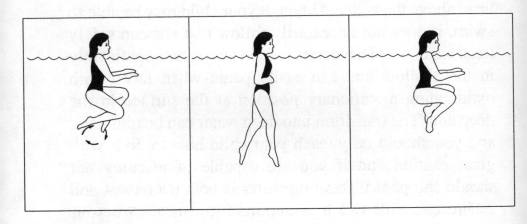

Treading water

the moves while in the shallow end, by getting your child to hold onto the rail and move into water just slightly out of her depth. Get her to move her legs in one of the ways outlined above and leave go of the rail for a few seconds. Continue this until she is confident at being only slightly out of their depth and close to the rail.

Next, enter the pool with your child at the deep end and move along the rail with her. Get your child to hold onto the rail with one hand and onto a float with the other and attempt each leg action. Make sure she changes her hands on the rail and practises on both sides. When she is confident with these movements, repeat the exercise but without the float. This time get your child to use her free hand to make the front paddle action.

To progress, then get your child to hold a float under each arm and practise the leg movements. Once the leg and arm actions have been mastered, encourage your child to do the two together, next to the rail, while you hold onto the rail beside her. As she gradually increases the amount of time she is treading water, her confidence will grow.

FURTHER WATER SKILLS

Once the child is confident in the water and is ready for more formalised instruction, it is advisable to seek professional help by enrolling her in a series of lessons. It is important not to introduce the proper strokes too soon as your child will not have the strength to perform them successfully. Some children are ready as early as four or five years, but generally most are six. They should be able to paddle ten metres and be happy on both their front and their back. They should also be happy about going under water. At about six they will generally have the concentration and comprehension necessary to learn the three main strokes—front crawl, back crawl and breast stroke.

WHAT SWIMMING IS YOUR CHILD LEARNING AT SCHOOL?

From September 1994, the National Curriculum requires that "all pupils should swim at least 25 metres and demonstrate an understanding of water safety by the end of Key Stage 2 (11 years of age)".

Whilst it is hoped that the sheer love of activity in the water and the success achieved in learning to swim will be the major incentive for your child, it is recognised that children like to measure their progress. Your child can, therefore, through her school, be tested for the Amateur Swimming Association's National Curriculum Award (Water Skills), for which she will obtain a certificate and a badge. Schools are aware of this and are likely to be working towards it as the recording and monitoring of performance is an integral part of a child's development in all aspects of the school curriculum.

The test comprises three parts. **Test A** will require your child to start in the water, swim 25 metres in an efficient manner, though not necessarily using a recognised stroke, but certainly using both arms and legs. **Test B** requires the child to tread water or float for a minimum of 30 seconds to include full rotation to a vertical or horizontal (face up) position.

Finally, **Test C** requires the child to submerge their body totally under water and surface to face the examiner. If you are at all unsure about the swimming your child is doing at school, don't hesitate to ask her teacher.

WHO IS QUALIFIED TO TEACH YOUR CHILD TO SWIM PROFICIENTLY?

Any parent who can swim and is confident in the water can certainly take their child swimming, teach her confidence skills, and prepare her for the basic strokes. However, do remember that it is important that your child learns the strokes properly as bad habits can be difficult to undo.

Even if your child is learning swimming at school, it is worth enrolling her in swimming lessons at the local pool. Your child will learn good stroke technique and you will be able to watch the lesson and help your child practise what she has learnt. Individual lessons will be more expensive than group ones, and from your child's point of view, a lot less fun. Obviously, the smaller the class, the more attention your child will receive—less than ten in a class is preferable.

Swimming lessons normally last around 30 minutes and you may be asked to enrol and pay for a group of lessons in advance. Although lessons normally take place once a week during term time, crash courses are often organised for school holidays and these tend to achieve good results as your child will be swimming every day for one or two weeks.

Any swimming teacher actively involved in teaching children to swim should have a recognised qualification from the Amateur Swimming Association. The minimum qualification they should hold is the ASA Teacher Certificate (Swimming). Such an instructor is qualified to teach groups, normally consisting of between 8–16 participants of a range of ability from the non-swimmer through to those involved in early competition.

Those instructors holding the ASA Assistant Teacher Certificate (Swimming) are only able to assist in a swimming class, under the supervision of a qualified ASA teacher or coach. Don't be afraid to ask for proof of the instuctor's qualification before enrolling your child on a course, as it is your child's safety that is on the line. Qualified instructors will have undertaken a comprehensive training programme.

Qualifications aren't everything, however. Make sure that your child's instructor is also friendly and is at ease with children, but is capable of being firm when it matters. Above everything else, your child should come out of the water having had a good time and feel that she's made some improvement from the lesson before.

Now please read the KEY POINTS from chapter 2 overleaf.

KEY POINTS

- In order to get your child used to the water you should encourage her to play in the bath at home.

- Don't take your child into the water if she is suffering from a cold or other infections. Immunization is necessary before swimming lessons—a doctor will advise.

- From six months you can take your child to a pool.

- Check the depth of the water before you take your child in. Never turn your back on the child in the water.

- During the first few visits to the pool, allow your child to gain confidence and do not attempt to teach the child proper strokes in detail. Keep the sessions short to begin with.

- Your child should be encouraged to move freely in the water from as early as possible.

- Encourage your child to help herself out of the water.

- As your child comes to terms with water and begins to enjoy herself through activities, the need to teach more advanced swimming strokes will increase.

3

SAFETY ISSUES

It is time to reassess why you want your child to swim. Swimming is not just a recreation or a sport—it is a fundamental life saving skill.

SWIMMING AS A LIFE SAVING SKILL

Death by accidental drowning can usually be accounted for by the linking of several factors known as the drowning chain:

- ignorance, disregard or misjudgment of one's own ability;

- uninformed or unprotected access to the hazard;

- incompetent or non-present supervision, particularly of the young;

- an inability to cope once an emergency has arisen.

Although each link of the drowning chain can contribute to a fatality to a lesser or greater extent, the major cause of accidental drowning is attributed to the first point—ignorance, disregard or misjudgment of one's own ability.

The ability to swim is not enough to prevent the development of the drowning chain. Swimming in the relatively safe environment of an indoor swimming pool is far removed from being able to do so in cold, hostile open water, often against strong currents or tides or while fully clothed.

Eighty-five per cent of all accidental drownings in the UK occur each year at open water locations such as the sea, rivers, lakes, reservoirs and canals. It is essential that your child is made aware of the dangers of playing or swimming in or near open water.

In an attempt to overcome this problem, the Royal Life Saving Society UK and the Royal Society for the Prevention of Accidents have developed a joint Water Safety Code which is endorsed by the Amateur Swimming Association.

THE WATER SAFETY CODE

1. Spot the dangers—and avoid the hazard

2. Take safety advice—it is for your own good

3. Don't go it alone—'loners' live dangerously

4. Learn how to help—yourself, and others, if the worst
   happens

Your child will be taught the Water Safety Code from year
one at school, but do her a favour—make her aware of the
danger of water, and the hazards that can occur when
swimming in open areas.

SAFETY IN THE SWIMMING POOL

On a slightly less serious note, there are a number of
factors that you should consider for your child's safety
when you take her to the swimming pool. It would be a
good idea to talk to your child about these safety aspects
and make sure she understands the importance of good
behaviour in a pool environment.

Remember, be alert at all times!

Always keep your eyes on your child in the water.
Incidents happen in fractions of seconds, and turning your
back on the child, for whatever reason, can be dangerous.

Be aware of the following:

• The depth of the water and the area available in each

depth—make sure your child knows at exactly which point on the poolside she will no longer be able to touch the bottom;

- The abilities of your child and any other children you may take swimming;

- If you do take more than one child swimming, do you require extra help in supervising them?

- Any medical problem your child has that might affect her swimming. There are very few illnesses that should prevent your child from swimming, but if you are concerned, consult your health visitor or doctor for advice. If you or your child suffer from a medical condition such as asthma, epilepsy or a heart condition, but have your doctor's approval to swim, then always swim with a friend and discreetly make sure the staff at the pool know about your child's or your condition. You should not take your child swimming if she has a cold as this can quickly turn into a more severe upper respiratory infection or ear infection;

- The problems of swimming on a full stomach. Allow a reasonable time between eating and entering the water.

Swimming too soon after eating may cause a swimmer distress and may result in them being sick. Very young children should have something to eat some time in the hour before they go into the pool, but as children get older, and eat larger meals, they should leave an hour or so between a meal and a swim;

- The dangers of eating or chewing whilst in the pool— choking can very easily lead to drowning;

- The dangers of fooling around, running on the poolside, shouting in the pool, and throwing other children into the water. Such behaviour makes your child a danger to herself and to others in the pool;

- Your own swimming ability, strength and general fitness—if your child accidently paddles off towards the deep end of the pool, have you the strength or ability to go after her?

- Your life saving skills and those of any swimming pool attendants around you. Can you be of assistance in an emergency? If the answer is no, and you are a capable swimmer, perhaps you should think about enrolling in a life saving class;

• The rules and regulations that apply to the swimming pool you use, particularly about the conduct of children and the responsibilities of adults.

It is important to remember that all the exercises in this book are intended for use only in a controlled environment like a public swimming pool. The water is clear, you can easily watch your child and there are no unseen dangers such as rocks or strong currents which can be encountered in open water such as the sea, rivers, lakes, reservoirs and canals.

Because of these hazards, do not carry out any of the exercises described in this book in open water. Play safe and take your child to a swimming pool where there are qualified life savers and swimming pool attendants to help should an emergency occur. Do not be tempted to swim with your child, or encourage her to swim, in any open water.

Chapter 4 covers pool health, safety and hygiene in more detail and is intended for the would-be professional teacher.

Now please read the KEY POINTS from chapter 3 overleaf.

KEY POINTS

• Swimming is not only for personal enjoyment, it is also a fundamental life saving skill.

• Always keep your eyes on your child in the water.

• The ability to swim is not enough to prevent the development of the "drowning chain". It is essential that your child is made aware of the dangers of playing or swimming in, or near, open water.

• Your child will be taught the Water Safety Code at school from year one.

• Be aware of your child's medical condition before letting her swim. Be aware of other factors, such as eating cycles, before allowing your child to swim.

4

HEALTH, SAFETY & HYGIENE FOR THE PROFESSIONAL SWIMMING TEACHER

PERSONAL HYGIENE

A high standard of personal cleanliness is essential. Good habits must be learned by all from an early age and why they are necessary should be explained.

Feet should be frequently inspected and a teacher should be able to recognise the following two conditions:

- Athlete's foot. This infection may or may not be fungal, and is caused by excessive sweating between the toes, or lack of foot care.

- Verrucae. Warts on the sole of the foot are commonly known as verrucae and are catching by contact. Those infected must not be allowed to walk around in bare feet, either in the changing rooms or on the poolside. A plaster is not sufficient cover, and treatment to remove the wart should be arranged.

A child with either condition should not resume swimming until advised to do so by the doctor.

In addition, children suffering from the following should not be permitted to swim or to submerge in the water:

- colds, coughs, sore throats, nasal catarrh, acute sinusitis

- any discharge from the ears—this could be a middle ear infection

- skin infection, boils, burns, open wounds

- sore or inflamed eyes

- infectious diseases.

If there is any doubt, excuse the child from swimming and in appropriate cases ask for medical advice as to when the child can swim again.

SAFETY AND ORDERLINESS

Teaching and pool staff must have a thorough knowledge of safety procedures and action to be taken in an emergency, for example the location of the telephone, ringing for the ambulance, etc. Make sure children and adults are acquainted with regulations about hygiene and safety. Appropriate notices should be displayed in a prominent position.

SAFETY AND ORDER IN THE CHANGING ROOMS

• Children must be supervised before and after the lesson and orderliness must be established in the changing rooms.

• Glass bottles must not be allowed in the buildings (for example shampoo bottles). Broken glass is dangerous, particularly where people walk in bare feet.

• Make sure children do not enter the pool chewing gum or a sweet—make them remove it.

• Instruct children in the following routine before entering the pool:
  – visit the toilet
  – use a handkerchief to blow the nose
  – shower thoroughly to clean the body and feet
  – use the disinfectant footbath or wipe feet on the pads impregnated with disinfectant before entering the pool

• Towels should not be shared.

• Remind young children after the lesson to dry their hair,

eyes, ears and between the toes.

SAFETY ON THE POOLSIDE

- The deep and shallow ends of the pool should be clearly signed showing the depth of the water.

- Some authorities require an overall ratio of at least one adult to every twenty pupils. The teacher must be able to supervise all the pupils safely and teach effectively.

- On the first visit to the pool teachers and pupils should be made familiar with the pool alarm system.

- There must be at least one adult on the poolside at all times who is trained in life saving and methods of resuscitation. A teacher must at least know the location of the rescue equipment, resuscitator and first aid box.

- Where there is a history of a medical condition, consult the parent or doctor for advice before allowing the child to swim.

- Goggles should be checked as they can cause eye injuries. They are not normally necessary for swimming lessons, although they are used in training.

• Be familiar with any regulations laid down by the local Education Authority. Be aware of the guidance on water temperature.

SAFETY IN THE WATER

• Swimming should not take place within one hour after a meal.

• Pupils must not enter the water, or leave it, without permission.

• Insist on prompt obedience to signals. Establish a whistle drill, for example,
 – one blast 'Stop—Look—Listen'
 – two blasts 'Swim to the side, and stay in the water'
 – three blasts 'Get out of the water, and stand on the side'.

• Teachers in charge should not get in the water with pupils. If necessary, an additional teacher can be in the water to assist disabled or timid pupils.

- Pool discipline is vital, and a clear code of behaviour must be established. This will forbid running on the poolside, pushing in, bombing, ducking, rough play or shouting. Misbehaviour must be dealt with promptly and firmly.

- Use a partner system with each pupil having responsibility to keep an eye on a partner.

- Make sure a pupil can swim the required distance in shallow water without touching down, before the first attempt to swim a length, from deep to shallow.

- If the pool is crowded, with swimmers moving in different directions, collisions may occur, on the surface or under the water, causing head injuries. Fatalities can happen in these circumstances. Direction of movement can be controlled by wave swimming or chain swimming, with everyone swimming in the same direction.

- In lessons which involve undressing in the water, clothing should be placed on the poolside and not allowed to sink onto the pool floor.

- At the end of the lesson, make sure the whole class gets

out of the water, and after changing, check all are off the premises.

ARRANGEMENTS FOR STORING EQUIPMENT

Arrangements must be made for safely storing chemicals used in water treatment and cleaning the surrounds of the pool. Many of these chemicals are hazardous if handled inexpertly. When stored together, incompatible materials are potentially very dangerous and they must be separated by an incombustible screen.

Equipment is expensive, and must be locked away to avoid possible loss or damage, and should be distinctively marked. There are several useful systems for storing different articles of equipment but they should not cause obstructions or be potential hazards around the pool.

Now please read the KEY POINTS from chapter 4 opposite.

KEY POINTS

- It is essential in any swimming pool that a high standard of personal cleanliness is maintained.

- Regular inspection of feet is necessary before entry into the pool.

- All children and adults should be familiar with safety and hygiene regulations. These should be clearly displayed. All teaching/pool staff must have a thorough knowledge of safety procedures.

- Teachers in charge should not enter the water with pupils.

- Teachers should be able to administer first aid treatment if required.

- Proper facilities should be available for the storage of chemicals used in water treatment and cleaning.

5

OTHER WATER SPORTS FOR YOUR CHILD TO ENJOY

By learning to swim, your child can now confidently and safely take part in a wide range of water sports. Some are more demanding than others in terms of the strength and swimming ability they require, but if your child likes the water, think about encouraging her to try one of the sports below.

DINGHY SAILING

Messing about in boats is an excellent hobby, and thanks to the huge number of lakes and rivers and the miles of shoreline in and around Britain, it's a very accessible sport for everyone—provided they are a reasonably strong swimmer and don't panic in the water. Most sailing clubs generally run beginners and childrens classes at the weekends. Check out your local newspaper or library, or contact the national governing body, for the nearest club to you.

WINDSURFING

Windsurfing has enjoyed an incredible increase in popularity over the past few years, mainly due to the fact that it is an exhilarating, satisfying and colourful sport. By starting on a calm piece of inland water children as young as seven can enjoy the excitement windsurfing can generate. Your child will have to be a reasonably strong swimmer and be happy falling into the water to enjoy the sport. Again, check out your local newspaper or library, or contact the national governing body, for the nearest club to you.

CANOEING

Canoeing is one of the most exhilarating ways of enjoying the water. Your child can enjoy a leisurely paddle on a local pond, or, when they're more experienced, the thrills and spills of white water. Again, this sport demands that your child is a reasonably strong swimmer who won't panic if they fall in the water. Most clubs have junior and family members and run beginners courses for all ages and sexes. Contact the national governing body of the nearest club to you.

SURFING

True surfing, out in the sea, amongst the largest waves, requires a high degree of swimming competence. Your child must be able to swim strongly to get over the crashing surf and to cope with the biggest of tumbles.

However, there are beginners and childrens courses at various venues around the country, particularly in Cornwall, and surfing can be exhilarating for a child or beginner on even the smallest of waves. For details of courses contact the national governing body.

6

SOURCES OF FURTHER INFORMATION

For information about learning to swim, swimming awards and competitive swimming contact:

Amateur Swimming Association
Harold Fern House
Derby Square
Loughborough
LE11 0AL
Tel: 01509 230431

Irish Amateur Swimming Association
House of Sport
Longmile Road
Dublin 12
Ireland
Tel: 010 353 1 501 739

Scottish Amateur Swimming Association
Holmhills Farm
Greenlees Road
Cambuslang
Scotland G72 8DT
Tel: 0141 641 881

Welsh Amateur Swimming Association
Wales Empire Road
Wood Street
Cardiff CF1 1PP
Tel: 01223 42201

Information on life saving
Royal Life Saving Society
Mountbatten House
Studley
Warwickshire B80 7NN
Tel: 015278 53943

Contact the Leisure Services Department of your local authority to find out about swimming pools in your area. Their number will be in the telephone directory. You may also find the same information in your local newspaper.

For information on other watersports contact the relevant governing body.

CANOEING
British Canoe Union
John Dudderidge House
Adbolton Lane

West Bridgford
Nottingham NG2 5AS

SAILING & WINDSURFING
Royal Yachting Association
RYA House
Romsey Road
Eastleigh
Hants SO5 4YA

WATER SKIING
British Water Ski Federation
390 City Road
London EC1V 2QA
Tel: 0171 833 2855

SURFING
British Surfing Association
T2, Champions Yard
Penzance
Cornwall TR18 2SS
Tel: 01736 60250

OTHER BOOKS IN THIS SERIES

A STRAIGHTFORWARD GUIDE TO DIVORCE AND THE LAW

This book is the third in the current series of Straightforward Guides. Hopefully it will benefit your understanding of the law underpinning the process of divorce and help ease the difficult road ahead.

A STRAIGHTFORWARD GUIDE TO COMPUTING AND INFORMATION TECHNOLOGY

The second in the series, this book is designed to help and assist those who have yet to master the basics of computing and want a basic introduction to the subject.

A STRAIGHTFORWARD GUIDE TO THE RIGHTS AND OBLIGATIONS OF THE PRIVATE TENANT

This book is designed both for the person who is experiencing problems with his or her landlord, and for the student of housing law. It provides invaluable advice and information concerning the whole area of privately rented property.

FORTHCOMING STRAIGHTFORWARD GUIDES

A Straightforward Guide to Small Claims in the County Court

A Straightforward Guide to Residential Leases and the Law

A Straightforward Guide to the Management of Property

A Straightforward Guide to Handling Bereavement

A Straightforward Guide to Employment Law

A Straightforward Guide to Personal Finance

A Straightforward Guide to Women in Soccer

A Straightforward Guide to Modern Car Maintenance

A Straightforward Guide to Producing an Effective C.V.

A Straightforward Guide to Setting up Your Own Business

If you would like to see any particular subject produced in the Straightforward Guide Series please do not hesitate to contact us at: 38 Cromwell Road, Walthamstow, London E17 9JN.

INDEX

INDEX

T
Teacher (swimming), 47, 60–66

W
Warts, 60
Water Safety Code, 53
Water sports, 70–71
Windsurfing, 70